Curé d'Ars

Saint John Vianney

by
George William Rutler

All booklets are published thanks to the
generous support of the members of the
Catholic Truth Society

CATHOLIC TRUTH SOCIETY
PUBLISHERS TO THE HOLY SEE

Contents

The early years

Ars-sur-Formans is a village in southeast France, just 40 kilometers from Lyons. It was difficult to find in 1818, when the priest John Mary Vianney, in his early thirties, arrived with a few possessions, mostly books, in a cart. One item he had, which he kept all his life, was the shaving mirror of his own parish priest, Charles Balley of nearby Ecully, who Vianney believed was a saint. He was good at seeing saints in others, and said with awe that the mirror "had reflected the good priest's face." A young local boy named Antoine Givre pointed out the village to Vianney, not that there was much to see in the settlement of about 260 people, four taverns and a broken down church. Vianney thanked Antoine: "You have shown me the road to Ars. I shall show you the road to Heaven." It was an odd remark, and the new pastor said it matter-of-factly, but the boy always remembered it.

Harsh times

Vianney was not much taller than five feet and thin, his hair longish and his features angular. He wore rough shoes and an ill-fitting cassock made of coarse wool for hard work. There would be much work. The Vicar General had told him: "There is not much love of God in that parish; you will bring some into it." It was not large enough to qualify as a parish with a proper pastor. Since the Revolution, two priests in charge had abandoned it, and one had died in the unhealthy climate. For a while the tiny church had been turned into a kind of lodge for a small group who called themselves Freethinkers, although they were not quite sure what that meant. On his first day, he tried to ring the broken bell but it only clanked and no one showed up for Mass.

The dismal scene was the product of a long neglect of the Faith which went far back beyond the chaos of the Revolution. But those recent harsh years which tore the fabric of France with high-sounding hopes had turned into a terror, and had proscribed the Catholic life of the land. By the time of Napoleon's pragmatic restoration of official Catholicism, religious practice had largely evaporated. The sadness was worsened by the defeat of France's Grand Army. Families were broken, and the byways were filled with homeless children. The taverns offered quick and fleeting solace, and the traditional festivals turned raucous, for attempts at simple fun had failed. Vianney was no prude, but he knew the occasional public dances for what they were – lame and lewd.

Growing up in the Revolution

He had been born in a farmhouse in Dardilly on 8th May 1786 and lived as a farm boy, but with an intuition of a different life. One priest has unsuccessfully tried to introduce the ways of the puppet church, independent of the papacy, which had been set up by the Civil Constitution of the Clergy. But even the untutored local people had sensed that something was wrong because he did not say thanksgiving prayers after Mass. Hundreds of priests who refused to conform died as galley slaves, some as far away as Guyana. A few faithful priests ministered occasionally in disguise. One of them, Monsieur Groboz heard the eleven year old Jean-Marie's confession "at the foot of our clock." Mass was said from time to time in barns with local farmers keeping guard. That is how he made his first Communion two years later, with fifteen other children.

Dechristianisation

All the while, the people heard the reports of mass executions at the guillotine in Lyons under the cold direction of Joseph Fouché, who had studied with the Oratorians in Nantes and Paris and taken Minor Orders before becoming one of the Revolution's architects of 'dechristianisation,' personally slaughtering 130 priests with an efficiency that amazed even Robespierre.

Originally the guillotine had been promoted by a physician, Guillotin, an opponent of capital punishment, as a humane attempt to improve the clumsier methods. Louis XVI had once formed a scientific commission made up of him along with Antoine Lavoisier, who had promoted Jenning's practice of vaccinations, and Benjamin Franklin, to disprove the quack theories of Mesmer. Guillotin was imprisoned by the Terror but survived and helped found the Academy of Medicine in Paris. Lavoisier was decapitated by the Republic which declared that the Revolution had "no need of science." Fouché, after a tumultuous time as Minister of Police for Napoleon who disdained him but found him useful, died in Trieste in restless exile in 1820.

Vianney survived childhood in those twisted times but never forgot them. He said that a priest is a man who would die to be one. He would also say from hard experience, "When one wants to destroy religion, one begins by attacking the priests."

Vocation

While working dutifully on the family farm, Vianney was convinced that he was called to be a priest. When he had his own parish he would often tell the people, "When you see a priest you should say: 'There is the one who has made me a child of God…one who has cleansed me from my sins, who gives nourishment to my soul.'" It was not a complete impossibility since Napoleon had ended the Revolution's prohibitions in 1802 with his Concordat legalising the Church under papal obedience. Napoleon had his own pragmatic reasons, but he knew France needed the Church and so did he.

The local bishop had instructed priests to start classes for pre-seminary training and Father Balley did so in the local parish. Vianney enrolled, but as a teenager he was the oldest and the younger children made sport of him as he sat cramped behind a small desk. Once, when he could come up with the right answer, a boy named Loras punched him. Vianney knelt and apologised, which shamed Loras to tears. "The way to be truly wise, my children, is to accept everything as coming from the hand of God." That boy Loras eventually would become a missionary bishop across the ocean in Iowa, and so fine a one that when he died he was considered a saint.

Vianney had difficulty learning to read, and tried to help himself by fasting, sometimes for two or three weeks. Later he would call that a folly of his youth. He was not the dullard that some biographers have called him. He was just not used to using his brain in an academic way. He reverenced books as rare and almost magical tools. Latin was as exotic as it was difficult.

Cardinal Fesch, an uncle of Napoleon and Archbishop of Lyons confirmed Vianney in 1807. It was not uncommon for him to confirm thousands in a single day to make up for the lost years. From that time Vianney began to sign himself as Jean-Marie-Baptiste or Jean-Baptiste-Marie. In a dark moment when he thought he might give up his priestly ambition, he made a pilgrimage to the shrine of Saint Francis Regis who had done much to teach Catholicism when Protestantism first began to spread. Vianney was inscribed as a candidate for Holy Orders in his twenty-first year.

Soldier

Napoleon showed his peculiar attitude to religion by seizing the Papal States and arresting the Pope in 1809. Vianney's limited studies were not enough to persuade the authorities that he was a serious seminarian and he was enlisted in the army for the Spanish campaign. He was not a pacifist and, with all Frenchman he honoured the armoured saints Louis IX and Joan of Arc.

The new soldier contracted fever and spent eight weeks in two military hospitals and then was ordered off to Spain, although he had no uniform and no training in manoeuvres. An officer flung a knapsack at him and ordered him to catch up with the rear guard in Renaison. "Never, perhaps, have I said the rosary with such courage". Lost on the road and exhausted, he was led by a woodsman to the hamlet of Les Robins where he was told to hide because he was already considered a deserter.

He spent two years working with the farmers, both terrified that he was a criminal, and managing to charm to the local people. If naïve about the ways of the government, he was also innocent of evil intent. His own family had no word of his whereabouts. He was certainly not, as his greatest admirers said, a draft-dodger. Soon the number of *réfractaires* outnumbered the active enlistees. When a general amnesty was granted in 1810 to celebrate the Emperor's marriage to his new wife, the Archduchess Marie-Louise, the citizens of Les Robins found black cloth to stitch together a soutane. He referred to those days only once late in life, when he was amused and not a little perplexed that Napoleon III sent him a medal.

Seminarian

A few weeks after he returned home, his mother died. "I can never think of her without weeping." In 1812, the 26 year old was sent to the minor seminary at Verriers. He got high marks in zeal, conduct and character but was listed as very weak in 'general knowledge'. At the Major Seminary in Lyons he felt despair when it came time to take the examinations. A classmate said, "There was nothing extraordinary about Jean-Marie. He was just perfectly simple." The faculty were not impressed by that and dismissed him after six months with the lowest grade they could give.

Conquering depression, he resolved to become a lay brother in some institute but, back home, Monsieur Balley gave him a crash course and presented him for another examination. His mind went blank, but the faculty agreed to recommend him for Minor Orders if he could find a bishop who would take him. Balley asked the chief examiner, Canon Bouchard, to test him on his familiar turf in Ecully, and in French rather than Latin. The people lit candles in the church during the examination. "Monsieur Balley was a saint. But there is one thing he will have to answer for before God, and that is having me admitted to Holy Orders." The Canon was impressed.

Ordination as priest

In 1813 the Emperor abdicated and Cardinal Fesch fled. In the confusion, the Vicar General summoned him to ordination and said the grace of God would do the rest. On the Feast of the Visitation in 1814 he received Minor Orders in the cathedral of Lyons. One priest watching said, "He is less learned than many of his companions, but he will do far more than they in the sacred ministry." At the next examinations, "our theologian," as one of the examiners wryly called him, did very well. He headed off to priestly ordination in Grenoble along a dirt road one hot August day, with some food and an alb.

On 12th August 1815 Bishop Simon laid hands on his head and anointed him. "How great is the priest! The priest will only be understood in heaven. Were he understood on earth, people would die, not of fear, but of love." The next day, he offered his first Mass unnoticed as two Austrian army chaplains said Mass at nearby altars.

"The priest should have the same joy as the apostles in seeing our Lord whom he holds in his hands." The trip to Grenoble and home again was the longest he would ever make. "At the sight of a steeple you can say, what's that in there? The body of our Lord. Why is he there? Because a priest has passed by and said the Holy Mass."

A Parish changed

Because of his tentative learning, the priest who would spend most of his waking hours hearing confessions was denied faculties as a confessor for several months. His first penitent was his own parish priest, Monsieur Balley, who took him on as his curate since no one else would have him. His sister Marguerite visited Ecully from Dardilly and admitted that he did preach very well. Others said that he had St Francis de Sales' gift for "seeing everyone without looking at anyone."

Confessions were difficult for him, as he had little experience of the temptations and failings he began to confront in the confessional. To steady himself, each day he said the "*Regina Coeli*" and recited six times: "Blessed be for ever the most holy and Immaculate Conception of the Blessed Virgin Mary, Mother of God! Amen."

His parish priest took him on frequent pilgrimages to the shrine of Our Lady of Fourvière. Vianney anointed him in 1817 when he was dying from gangrene. "Look, my poor child," said Balley as he handed Vianney his instruments of penance, "hide these things; if they were found after my death people would imagine that I have sufficiently expiated my sins, and so they would leave me in purgatory until the end of the world." Vianney knew better, which is why he kept that mirror.

Appointed to Ars

The parishioners of Ecully wanted the young priest as their pastor but the authorities doubted his competence for even so modest a parish, and so did Vianney: "I would not have liked to be the parish priest of Ecully; it was too big a parish." A new pastor, Monsieur Tripier, thought Vianney was 'rigid' and furnished the presbytery in a more comfortable fashion.

When the undesired parish of Ars in the Ain region became available, Vianney was assigned there. So he arrived in 1818, welcomed by no one save the kindly lady of its chateau who wanted a chaplain. He arrived on 9th February in a cold mist, his tricorner hat under his arm, and was the only man in the world who looked on Ars with promise. The small church of weathered greyish-yellow stone was surrounded by a few thatched cottages. Rumour had it that a man named Ruf had tried to make it a Temple of Reason during the Revolution. Vianney said to himself, "How small it all is. Yet this parish will not be able to contain the multitude of those who shall journey here."

Bold beginnings

Of the fifty or so families in Ars, only a few showed any interest in the church or its God, but they showed up for the new Curé's installation a week later. He was in his thirty-second year but felt much older, eighteen hundred years older, when the former superior of the minor seminary led him from the small two-storey presbytery into the church and placed the stole on his shoulders. At two o'clock the next morning, one of the locals went into the church out of curiosity and found the new Curé d'Ars on his knees. People began to whisper, "This one is not like the others." His sallow and sunburned face looked prematurely wrinkled, but many who tilled the soil were that way. The next Sunday he seemed to skip into the pulpit and preached in a sharp and tinny voice which the *chatelaine*, Madame des Garets, said always hurt her ears. His opening was not a study in charm: "Christ wept over Jerusalem ... I weep over you. How can I help weeping, my brethren. Hell exists. It is not my invention. God has told us. And you pay no heed ..."

Effects of puritanism

The puritanical spirit of Jansenism had filled the void of religious sentiment in those who tried to make sense of God in those cynical times. Jansenism, as a school of theological thought, had spread in France in the sixteenth century until Pope Clement XI condemned it in 1713. As a general psychological climate, it continued to shape attitudes. Its distinction between an ideal 'Spiritual Church' and a barely tolerated 'Institutional Church' sat well with the Gallican sense of superiority to Rome. Its liturgical attitudes, which would turn the Mass into an edification of the people more than a worship of God, was congenial to the puritan whose severe spirituality wanted to strip the churches of any embellishments that evoked a mystery beyond human grasp.

When Pope John Paul II visited Ars in 1986, he commented about the dangers of rigorism which did not understand the Divine Mercy. In dim times it was easy to think that Original Sin had hopelessly condemned the human race and that misery is our lot. In the Jansenistic calculation, sinfulness obscured redemption. The spiritual infection was as corrosive as the complacency which, in more comfortable times, obscures the reality of sin altogether.

Vianney had absorbed some of that angularity. He struggled against it because he never lost confidence in the Divine Love who made the world.

Mercy

Like Dr Johnson who could not be a philosopher because cheerfulness kept breaking through, Vianney's happiness with God was more contagious than the infection of scrupulosity. He became more and more like St Alphonsus Liguori in the confessional, giving light penances and doing the rest himself. Penitents were told, "Well, my child, say such and such a prayer and forget all that." In 1828 he demurred when his bishop wanted him to become parish priest of Fareins which had a history of Jansenism: "Pagans are more quickly converted than Jansenists."

Confessions rediscovered

The confessional became the engine for the revival of Ars. Soon Vianney would spend up to sixteen hours a day hearing confessions as pilgrims flocked. He was intent on the redemption of souls, rather than just their reformation.

Inaugurating the Year for Priests in 2009, Pope Benedict XVI said: "Priests ought never to be resigned to empty confessionals or the apparent indifference of the faithful to this sacrament. In France, at the time of the Curé of Ars, confession was no more easy or frequent than in our own day, since the upheaval caused by the Revolution had long inhibited the practice of religion. Yet he sought in every way, by his preaching and his powers of persuasion, to help his parishioners to rediscover the meaning and beauty of the sacrament of Penance, presenting it as an inherent demand of the Eucharistic presence." The Pope chose to start the Year for Priests on the Feast of the Sacred Heart, which devotion had been anathema to the Jansenists, for Vianney had preached over and over: "The priesthood is the love of the heart of Jesus."

Hidden holiness

Vianney was 'a real character' but not in the superficial sense of eccentricity as it is commonly meant. A 'character' is an imprint, and Vianney was imprinted with the love of God in a way that made others want to be impressed by it themselves. In later testimony, a youth of those early days, Guillaume Villiers, insisted: "The majority judged him to be full of kindness, cheerfulness, and affability, though we never realised his great holiness." True to form, Vianney said, "If one of the damned could just say once 'My God, I love you' it would no longer be hell for him." By the end of his life, over 80,000 pilgrims came each year, from as far as America, to be close to him. One year, the figure claimed was 120,000. Vianney did not count numbers because one soul is worth the entire universe: "Only on the Day of Judgment will one know how many souls were saved in Ars."

Pastoral ways

His own parishioners were his first responsibility. When he arrived in Ars, he wrote all their names on a ribbon and placed it in a gilt metal heart attached to a statue of the Blessed Mother. Many of those inscribed did not return the compliment at first. They deeply resented his criticisms of their barn dances which were virtual debauches, and his cold eye on the absinthe drinkers who were ruining their families and themselves. "We live in such a poor century. Although it may seem grand, think about its poverty and its opulence."

The Curé was accused by some of morbid austerity and, inconsistently, of fathering a child by a derelict woman. He kept preaching, sometimes falling asleep in the sacristy over books of the ancient Fathers whom he tried to interpret to the people, having struggled first with them himself. He would sometimes preach for nearly an hour, and defended the assistant priest he was finally given, when a neighbouring priest said he preached too long: "He puts them into an ecstasy but you do not even give them time to sit down." In his first years he tried to memorise his sermons but his memory was poor. When he lost his train of thought he would sink down in the pulpit like a drowning man. In his last years, when he was almost toothless, and practically incomprehensible, the congregation thought he was the most eloquent, as he kept pointing to the Tabernacle: "He is there! He is there!"

Preaching missions

When the grand Dominican orator Lacordaire heard in Paris of the man in Ars, he visited and preached from the rickety pulpit which was such a contrast to the pulpit of his conferences in the cathedral of Notre Dame. Vianney was bewildered: "How is it that the greatest in science should come to me, the weakest?" If Lacordaire indulged histrionics on occasion, he was not a sentimentalist. So

Vianney was astonished that there were tears in Lacordaire's eyes when he stood in the poor pulpit of Ars.

Because of a priest shortage, Vianney was one of the priests directed to give missions in other obscure parishes in the department of the Ain: Trevoux, Saint-Trivier-sur-Moignans, Limas, and Chaniens. At Trevoux in 1823, the rush of penitents nearly overturned his confessional. Once he nearly fainted from hunger and was thought to be dying. Sometimes he was forced to take a carriage if he seemed to be faltering, but he usually walked from parish to parish.

On entering the church in Limas: "I beheld the chancel full of clergy and the body of the church packed with people of every condition. At first I felt unnerved by the spectacle. However I began to speak of the love of God, and apparently everything went well: everybody wept."

Works of mercy

All of Fareins poured out to greet him in 1837 when he arrived to absolve a woman dying of cancer. Another time, he lay down to hear the confession of sick man, as he was sicker than the man himself. Beggars knew he would give them his own clothes and once he returned to Ars without his shoes.

Baptisms, confessions and communions increased in Ars, even though frequent communion was still a rare custom in the universal Church. This threatened those accustomed to indifference. More than a few called him a bore and, resenting the way regular Mass attendance was once again becoming the norm, they yawned loudly during his sermons. He would stop and sigh: "When I am with you I do not feel weary."

Jealousy and persecution

The Revolution of 1830, though comparatively mild in its consequences, stirred some to try to return Ars to its former ways. The younger ones who missed the promiscuous dances flung excrement at the presbytery and vandalised it for some eighteen months. "I thought a time would come when people would rout me out of Ars with sticks, when the bishop would suspend me, and I should end my days in prison. I see, however, that I am not worthy of such grace."

Of great help were a few women, headed by his housekeeper Catherine Lassagne, who helped him start a small school, La Providence, for children who were orphaned in the social turmoil, and some of whom had been abused. He helped carry the bricks and mortar when it had to be enlarged to house about sixty children. When food ran out, he prayed and an upstairs room suddenly filled with so much grain that the floor almost shattered. The grain was not typical of the region. It was accounted an early miracle of Ars.

As clerical envy has not been lacking in any generation when the Holy Spirit is conspicuously at work, some clergy in the diocese circulated a petition for the removal of the Curé d'Ars on the grounds of his ignorance. They forgot that he was on the list of recipients. When it arrived in the mail, he read it, agreed with it, and signed it. Soon the same priests were going to Vianney for confession. "The good God is very good."

How he lived

As the leading lady of Ars, the Comtesse Marie-Anne Colombe Garnier des Garets, commonly known as 'Madame Ars,' tried to make life more comfortable for her new pastor by sending furniture to the presbytery, which he politely returned. Her chateau, with twelfth century foundations, was not grand and she lived rather simply, devoted to charitable works. Vianney became her spiritual director, not satisfied with just receiving her philanthropy. Her devotions reflected the Jansenist flavour of her finishing school at St Cyr, and Vianney set out to correct that. He had good material with which to work: she had the sense of humour which is evidence of humility, and her family had bravely hosted hidden Masses during the Reign of Terror. She became his defender against the calumnies which stung him like bees throughout his life. Another beneficiary of his direction was the young Pauline Jaricot of Lyons whose influence on countless millions as foundress of the Society for the Propagation of the Faith abounds to this day.

Self-discipline

Vianney's rigorous self-discipline could not be hidden, however much he tried. It is easy to misunderstand his asceticism as neurotic and even pathological, if mortification of selfish desires is assumed to be inhibiting and motivated by self-loathing. His psychological balance and common sense proved his sanity. We might understand his rigours better if we thought of him as a spiritual athlete in training for a very great contest. "I make up in my flesh what is still lacking in regard to Christ's afflictions, for the sake of his body, which is the Church." (*Col* 1:24) He ate very little: a few potatoes and some milk each day, and once in a while a simple flour snack, called a *maitfaim*.

He did not make the mistake of mortifying others with his own mortifications, entertaining guests as finely as his circumstances permitted. His cooking pot and the bowl from which he ate are preserved as kind of natural cousins to his sacred vessels used on the altar. More remarkable was his ability to live habitually on two hours of sleep and patiently to hear upwards of sixteen hours of confessions day and night, in weather frigid and steamy. Patience was a practical fruit of these mortifications. Five years before his death, he could say, "Good gracious! I have spent thirty-six years in Ars and I have never been cross, and now I am too old to begin."

There was an irony in his fasts, for the greatest of French chefs, Brillat-Savarin, was born in the city of Belley. The Lyonnais region was the gastronomic capital of France and the heart of the nation's finest agricultural produce. He was eager to help the farmers with their harvests. Ten years before Vianney's death, a physician said that "science could not explain how he survived." His own answer was simple: "When you are working for heaven, you don't die of starvation."

Daily routine

The daily schedule, year in and out, seldom varied. It began at one in the morning when he walked through the dark with his lantern from the presbytery. From then until six he heard the women's confessions. After Mass at six there was a private thanksgiving and then he mingled with parishioners and visitors, chatting cheerfully. Then he went to La Providence at eight for a small cup of milk. At half past eight he began the men's confessions behind a screen in the sacristy. He found it more efficient to keep the men and women apart for these sessions. Until then it had not been common for men to confess at all. When one man whom he had never met confessed that he had been away from the sacrament for forty years, the Curé corrected him: "Forty-four". The befuddled man took a pencil and figured it out on the plaster wall that he was right.

Visitors and reading

At ten there was a break for public prayers and then more confessions until eleven when he went to La Providence to instruct the children, stopping for the Angelus at noon. As the crowds grew over time, it took a quarter of an hour to work his way across the square to the presbytery for the bite of food he called lunch. He talked to visitors while eating, standing all the while. He never let anyone stand out of respect for him except in the liturgical rites. This was a chance for some banter: he liked to tell jokes.

Rarely did he glance at a newspaper and comment on events of the day. Of public events he new enough to predict that Napoleon III "would one day be an enemy of the Church". When a Carlist officer in 1849 complained out of earshot about the new "liberal Pope," Vianney searched for him that afternoon and told him that "Pius IX will be one of the greatest Popes that ever ruled the Church." He did read in bed, of necessity briefly, and it is said that his one recreational reading was the *Annals of the Society of Propagation of the Faith*, which few would call diverting.

He had no idea what Paris was like, or any other city for that matter. But he did speak of the Pope in Rome as though they were old friends. Then he visited the sick and dying and, in a village with little medicine, this was a daily work. The knots of people who accompanied him could be vexing. When someone appeared with scissors to snip a bit of his hair as a living relic, the Curé stared at him sadly, but later admitted: "I nearly boxed his ears."

End of the day

Vespers and Compline were followed by women's confessions until six and the men until eight. Evening prayers and the Rosary were led from the pulpit. Confessions usually followed until ten or sometimes midnight. He was back at work at one. He never took a day off and his bishop imprudently would not allow him to make a retreat, saying that he did not need one. This was the normal routine seven says a week for thirty years.

When asked if he longed for heaven, he answered that he would put it off for a while: "In heaven the saints are happy indeed, but they are like men who live on their income. They have laboured well, for God punishes laziness and only rewards work; however, unlike ourselves, they cannot by their labours and sufferings win souls for God."

Some thought he had perfected a sense of smell: like a hound, the saint was known to sniff out the lapsed when they tried to hide from him. He startled one farmer who was couched in a haystack and led him by his arm into the church. If anyone felt sorry for his hardships, he would respond that the worst cross is to have no cross.

Alcoholism was the drug problem of his day, and when a tavern keeper complained that the Curé's temperance sermons were bad for his business, Vianney agreed and helped buy the man a farm.

Convert my parish

The daily toil took its toll, but not just physically. He complained that he did not have the solitude to be with God. His chief temptation was to leave Ars for a monastery. He tried three times to sneak away from the village, the last in 1853, and each time the people carried him back in a kind of triumph. He finally surrendered, blessing the people, "My God, here is all – take all: but convert my parish. If you do not convert my parish it is because I have not deserved it."

Given how hard he was on himself, it is striking how easy he was on others, except hypocrites and the superficially pious. When one woman of flowery piety batted her eyes and purred for advice on how to get to Heaven, he answered curtly: "Quite straight. Like a cannonball." He told another that February was her best month because it gave her one less day for gossip.

As his mortifications were for the sake of the parish, there was a logic to his gentleness with sincere souls. He made prayer seem simple: "Prayers are like two friends living together." Farm boys could be seen praying the Rosary at their ploughs, and as early as 1830 he rejoiced from the pulpit: "Ars is no longer Ars!". The master of prayer lets others teach him. A favourite of his stories was one about Louis Chaffangeon who was deep in prayer each day in the church. "What are you doing here all this time?" The farmer replied "*J' avise le bon Dieu et le bon Dieu m' avise.* (I look at the good God and the good God looks at me.)"

Miracles

Miracles are the evidence of holiness and not holiness itself. As with Christ, the Curé performed supernatural signs out of compassion, but not as stunts. And as they were signs pointing to heaven, they would have contradicted themselves if they had been distracting stunts. It was his device to ascribe his prodigies to his favourite saint, Philomena. Before blessing the sick, he would ask them why they wanted to be well. In a testimony of 1911, the great-nephew of blind Francoise Lebeau told how the Curé had said "My child, you can be cured, but if the good God restores your sight, your salvation will be less assured. If, on the contrary, you consent to keep your infirmity, you will go to heaven, and I guarantee that you will have a high place there." When she asked who would take care of her, he replied that her eight brothers and sisters would do that, and then in a nonchalant way he accurately predicted when each of them would die.

But he did heal the deaf and blind Claudine Venet, of Viregneux, on 1st February 1850. "Your eyes are healed, but you will become deaf for another twelve years. It is God's will that it should be so!" Her deafness suddenly returned, but at least she could see. On 18th January 1862, her hearing returned.

When crowds almost overwhelmed him, he announced that he had "forbidden" Philomena to work any more miracles: "It causes too much talk. I have asked the saint to cure souls here to her heart's content, but to heal bodies elsewhere." Evidently, Philomena did not listen. When a boy entered the church with a large tumour on his face, Vianney forgot the crowd that had gathered and touched the face. The tumour immediately disappeared. His assistant, Toccanier, said, "This time you won't say it was Philomena!" Vianney pushed his way through the excited group and ran out of the church: "How ashamed I was. If I could have found a rat hole, I should have hidden in it."

Catechism

Daily communion was a rarity in those days, but he promoted it, and often rounded up the men who were idling around the village square. Sunday Mass typically lasted from 8am until 11am. At one in the afternoon, clad in surplice, he entered a booth in the small nave and conducted the catechism for the children. On weekdays he instructed them at six in the morning in La Providence but by 1845 this was moved into the church because of the crowd of adults who wanted to listen. The instruction was basic and simple. "Worldly people say that it is too

difficult to save one's soul. Yet there is nothing easier:
keep the Commandments of God and the Church, and
avoid the Seven Deadly Sins; or, to put it another way, do
good and avoid evil. Here is a good rule of conduct. Do
only what one can offer to God." As far as confession
went, mentioning your sins to a priest was "taking the
nails out of Jesus."

As human beings are by definition creatures that
worship, Vianney was happiest at the altar. Mass was said
without affectation or dramatic pauses, though he
sometimes paused a while at the Consecration. He said
Mass like any other priest, although his church was
shabbier than most, having been badly renovated in
revolutionary times. He regretted that and set about to fix
it up. The one extravagance of Vianney was spending
money on furnishing the humble building. Noble
simplicity did not mean austerity. What little space there
was, he filled with shrines. To make a point about the
riotous street fairs, he placed over the shrine of St John
the Baptist: "He paid for a dance with his head."

His church

The longest trips he made were into Lyons, the silk
capital of the world, to buy vestments of the finest
workmanship. The Curé's artistic taste was untutored, so
he took the advice of experts. Left to his own devices,
there were lapses in decorative art. Towards the end, he

planned a lottery to enlarge the church. It was not finished when he died, and only the intervention of Pius X preserved the little nave. Vianney did not advertise poverty, and was ashamed to think that anyone would try to make God poor. As for music, he knew little of that, and was easily satisfied when the people sang with fervour. When a marching band showed up at one Corpus Christi procession, he visibly shook with delight. One account relates that he liked to enliven these processions with fireworks. As an older man he still carried the heavy gold monstrance for two hours in these processions and refused help: "Oh, why should I be tired? He whom I carried likewise carried me."

Spiritual combat

The chief strategy of Satan, as Anti-Christ, is to persuade people that he does not exist. That was remarked by a contemporary of Vianney, Father Ravignan and was updated by Pope Paul VI who spoke in 1972 of the "living, spiritual being" who contradicts God: "What are the greatest needs of the Church today? Do not let our answer surprise you as being over-simple or even superstitious and unreal: one of the greatest needs is defence from that evil which is called the devil."

Spirit of evil

Satan, haunter of the world, is haunted by holiness. His ordinary method is simple temptation. More rarely, he and his lesser evil spirits try to terrify by noise and moving objects. This is called 'infestation'. 'Obsession' is physical assaults of evil on a person, and 'possession' is the action of an evil spirit in and through one's consciousness. It was no surprise that Satan would hate Vianney and try to hurt him.

From 1824 until two years before his death, Vianney suffered both infestation and obsession, and occasionally confronted people who were possessed. The assaults seem to have begun when the school for children, La Providence, was under construction.

Two physicians who knew Vianney well, Dr Saunier and Dr Michel, attested to the saint's mental health. Sanctity, after all, means complete sanity. At first, the saint tried to ignore the infernal goings on in Ars. The banging sounds in the yard of the presbytery must have been burglars, he thought, though there was little to steal. He hired a strong 28 year old wheelwright as a night watchman. But after a few hours of loud rappings and the sound of carriage wheels racing through the house, and the floor shaking violently, the sturdy fellow left, much to the Curé's amusement. He hired others but they heard nothing. One night there was a sound of soldiers cursing, but they left no foot prints in the snow. Vianney said that God does not do that sort of thing: "I turn to God. I make the sign of the Cross. I address a few contemptuous words to the devil. I have noticed, moreover, that the tumult is greater and the assault more numerous if, on the following day, some big sinner is due to come."

Confidence in God

To deny the existence of evil is to give it strength; to worship evil is to succumb to it. "Because God did not make death, nor does he rejoice in the destruction of the living, the creatures of the world are wholesome. And there is not a destructive drug among them nor any domain of the nether world on earth, for justice is undying. It was the wicked who with hands and words invited death, considered it a friend, and pined for it, and made a covenant with it, because they deserve to be in its possession." (*Ws* 1:13-16)

Against the dualist heresy of the Manichaeans, who attributed creation to a demiurge, the Church responded with the sternness of a mother defending her young. In 1215, the Fourth Lateran Council taught: "God by his omnipotence, from the beginning of time, formed from nothing both types of creature, spiritual and corporal, that is angelic and earthly: and finally the human creature as made up of spirit and body, For the devil and the other demons were indeed created good by God, but by their own devices they became evil." Listening to the Curé confronting a devilish intruder was like hearing Saint Anthony in a similar encounter: "If you had any power, one of you would be sufficient. But Christ has hamstrung you, and so you try to frighten me by your numbers."

Always balanced

With holy nonchalance, and the wit which is evidence of moral balance challenging imbalance, Vianney nicknamed the devil a *grappin* which means a little rake which scratches. "The *grappin* is very stupid. He himself tells me of the arrival of big sinners." The scratchy voices persisted: "Vianney! Vianney! Potato eater! You are not dead! I shall get you alright!" At times the infestations became obsessions and felt like rats running over him, trying to toss him out of bed. Or the straw mattress suddenly felt soft and a voice began singing a lullaby. At those times the Curé would arrive for early Mass looking pale. Filth was flung at the engraving of the Annunciation over his bed. Vianney assured his sister: "He cannot hurt you. As for me he torments me in sundry ways. At times he seized me by the feet and drags me about the room. It is because I convert souls to the good God." One night when he was preaching a mission in Saint-Trivier, four witnesses heard shrill squeaks and watched his bed get tossed about and flung into the middle of the bedroom." A philosophy student named Denis Chaland was making his confession in the presbytery after spiritual direction: "Suddenly, when I was about half-way through my confession, a general convulsion shook the room; my *prie-Dieu* trembled like everything else. Full of terror I tried to stand up. Monsieur le Curé kept me down by seizing my arm. 'It is nothing,' he said, 'it is only the devil.'" After the absolution, Vianney told the young man he must become a priest, and eventually he did. "My excitement was still very great, and I must admit that I never again went to confession to the Curé d'Ars."

Ministering to the possessed

There were strange conversations, as once when a woman rushed at him shouting, "If there were three like you on earth, my kingdom would be destroyed. You have taken more than 80,000 souls from me." Vianney calmed her in a tender kind of exorcism. More violent was the case of Antoine Gay, a native of Lantenay, who was medically examined in 1843 at the request of the bishop of Grenoble and the archbishop of Lyons. After four months, the report found his ability to reveal lifelong secrets of his examiners to be inexplicable by natural analysis. From a mental asylum in Antiquaille, he was taken to Ars where he knelt before the Curé and, with a voice different from his own, cried: "Vianney, you are a thief! You are stealing from us the souls we had such difficulty in winning." Vianney made the sign of the Cross and the man shrieked. The man's condition seemed to worsen for a while, but he died in 1871 in a state of grace.

On 23rd January 1840, in the presence of eight witnesses, a manic woman challenged him in the renovated chapel of St John the Baptist: "You ugly black toad, how you make me suffer…You pass for an ignorant man. Why don't you preach like a great man, as they do in the towns? How I delight in those great sermons which do no harm to anyone, but leave the people to live their own way and do what they like." Soon after, at two in the morning, Vianney tried to walk away from Ars as fast as he could manage, but he stopped when he saw a pilgrimage cross which had been erected in the field of Les Combes. He turned around and slowly went home.

Temptation to leave

In 1843, afflicted with chronic neuralgia, gastritis and an attack of pneumonia from which he had barely recovered, he walked from Ars to his brother's house in Dardilly. Various parishioners followed him and begged him to return, and even the bishop intervened. His curate at the time, Monsieur Raymond, was considered better fit to run the parish and arranged for Vianney to go to a religious house in Beaumont. Vianney had already given his bedroom to Raymond and had begun sleeping in the kitchen. After one day, the Curé whispered, "God does not want me here." Having arrived by coach in Amerieux, he walked the rest of the way back to Ars leaning on a cane. Seeing the church tower he raised his arms: "I shall not leave you my children." He kept repeating the same to each of the bystanders who had gathered.

Those many years before, when he had been recruited into the army in the name of Napoleon, he had seemed a very poor soldier. Now he seemed scarred in another battle and bore the wounds with resignation. But just as some sort of peace seemed secured, there was one more skirmish. Ars had become accustomed to strangers arriving in the village at all times. But once, at midnight a coach pulled by two horses tore through the streets with a noise that awakened only the Curé who took his lantern to the door of the presbytery. A man put his hand on

Vianney's shoulder and said in a gentle voice, "Monsieur le Curé, if you wish to depart, we have a coach ready." The Curé stared at the figure's face, paused, and said "I have not the permission of my bishop." He removed the visitor's hand and hurried into the church. The figure was never seen again, nor was there any sound when the coach went away.

The last years

As the Church in France was rebuilding itself after the material and spiritual deprivation of the 1789 Revolution, she had a couple of advantages which made the renewal of his parish a bit easier for Vianney than it would have been in our day. There was a residual respect for the priesthood, built on the long native Catholic culture and enhanced by the sacrifices of priests in the days of persecution. The clergy were more learned than most citizens and performed various civil and social functions beyond their sacerdotal duties. There was also a general unity of doctrine and worship: widespread dissent on theological matters and liturgical confusion were absent. This is not to say that the nineteenth century was easy for the Faith. The resurgence of the Church provoked old anti-clerical resentments which would reach their apogee with the seizure of church properties and expulsion of Religious orders in 1906. When the Archbishop of Paris, Darbois, was shot by a firing squad in the Commune of 1871, he was wearing the cross and ring of two predecessors: Affre who was killed in the revolution of 1848, and Sibour who was assassinated two years before Vianney died.

As hard experience of the Terror had made the clergy cautious, their raw nerves did not welcome the singular events in Ars, and yet Vianney could not keep a low profile in spite of himself. But his bishop, Devie, told his clergy that, if they thought he was acting like some sort of wizard, he only wished they had some of is madness. The same Curé who could detect sin a mile away, had a pronounced reverence for other clergy, even when they criticised him. He was grateful for each of his bishops in succession and, when Devie died, he preserved one of the bishop's surplices and treated it as a relic.

Pilgrims increase

Once the pilgrims to Ars began to average three to four hundred daily, a special ticket window was opened in the main Lyons train station to sell eight-day tours, as that was how long it could take to get into the Curé's confessional. Small hotels were built, but Bishop Ullathorne of Birmingham saw large numbers sleeping in tents in the meadows. Vianney told Ullathorne that England would one day return to the Faith. Newman must have heard of Vianney from this good friend of his. On his deathbed in 1890, Newman asked that a biography of the Curé be read to him, and after a few pages he complained that the lush hagiography did not tell enough about the real man.

Heart of a prophet

Henri Ghéon wrote, "Freud, who explains everything by 'repression' would have to say that M. Vianney gave back to his environment immeasurably more life than he received from it." He did seem to have feet in two worlds, and made his own acre of the universe livelier for it. He approached in the church one grieving woman, whom he had never met and said smiling: "Do not worry. Between the bridge and the water your husband repented and made an act of contrition. Pray for him." As one man was making a perfunctory confession, he heard the Curé weeping and asked why: "I weep because you do not weep." One wealthy woman stopped by Ars out of curiosity on her return to Paris from her villa in the south of France. Vianney approached her outside the church and told her to follow him. In the church he told her that she was being prevented from confessing by the 'two devils' of pride and impurity. She was honest enough to agree and left for Paris. Eventually, she returned to her villa, which the Curé had described in detail, and was converted.

It was his style to open the door to the confessional with an elegant bow, like a footman. Sometimes he would go to one confessional and, when a line of penitents rushed to it, he would scurry across to the other box to hear those who had been too shy to swarm after him. For those who thought he was naïve, there were as many who thought he was cunning. A police inspector was dispatched to Ars in 1851 when ridiculous reports circulated in Lyons that he had predicted the assassination of the prince-president. The poor mayor of Ars was beside himself, and left the two together. After ten minutes in the sacristy, the inspector came out sobbing loudly: "Your Curé is wonderful. He is a saint." The police closed the investigation.

The Baronne de Lacomble made a three day trip to ask his advice when her eighteen-year old son was intent on what she considered to be an unsuitable marriage. The crowds were so great that she doubted she would get to speak with him, even after she finally had found a place in the rear of the church shortly before she had to leave. Suddenly the bent, white-haired figure came out of the confessional, walked down the nave directly to her. She was too stunned to speak as he whispered into her ear: "Let them marry. They will be very happy."

His curate

There have been times in the long history of Christianity when curates did not get on well with their parish priests. Vianney had helped his curate, Antoine Raymond through seminary and paid his tuition. Raymond thought he would replace Vianney at the time of the flight to Dardilly in 1843, and was not pleased when Vianney returned. The Curé allowed Raymond, who was twenty years younger, to dominate the pulpit even when he sometimes made jibes about him. When the Vicar General proposed removing Raymond, Vianney objected: "Let me keep him. He is not afraid to tell the truth about myself." Raymond was given another parish six years before the Curé died. To his credit, Raymond testified in the canonisation process and wrote a brief biography of his mentor, recalling what he had said as a child when he first saw Vianney in his schoolyard at Meximieux in 1822: "It is the holy Curé d'Ars!"

Aging

The Curé cut his hair short, thinking it might relieve his chronic headaches. His daily routine was unaltered, but he seemed older than his years and in 1855 he tried to walk part of the way to Dardilly as his brother François was dying, but was too weak and turned back. "The greatest cross is to have no cross." News of his brother's death came on Holy Saturday and he mourned quietly as he heard eighteen hours of confession without a pause. By this time, the children who remembered the early years in Ars were grown up, and he drew strength from them. "When you are with me, things are not so bad, but when I am alone, I am worth nothing… I am like the zeros that have no value except alongside some other figures."

The older he looked outside, the younger he seemed to become inside. The old spark was still there, even brighter. A self-important university student who required time to "discuss religion" was told, "You are an ignoramus, my friend." When a boy was sent by his mother to be scolded for not doing his homework, the Curé told him: "Play, my child. It is the privilege of your age." One day the new bishop, Chalandon, arrived with a retinue and declared him a canon, placing on his shoulders a mozetta of scarlet and crimson. The Comtesse des Garets, Mademoiselle d'Ars, said he looked a condemned man with a noose around his neck. With unfailing courtesy, Vianney thanked the bishop and, as soon as the dignitaries departed, he sold the cape for fifty francs. But in the same year, to celebrate the definition of the Immaculate Conception, he appeared in a fourteen hundred franc cope that he had specially commissioned.

Soon afterward, the Marquis de Castellane, sub-prefect of Trévoux, from mixed motives of reverence and practicality, wrote to Paris:

"In a small commune of my arrondisssement, the population of which numbers 510 souls, there is a clergyman whose evangelical holiness and lofty piety have gained him a European reputation… The commune of Ars, formerly the most obscure in my arrondissement, witnesses a daily influx of a prodigious number of pilgrims. Transport facilities had had to be organised; these have been functioning for a considerable time. This concourse, now of long standing and wholly due to the reputation for sanctity of a humble priest, constitutes a truly marvellous event in a century which has inherited so many doctrines that are anti-religious and hostile to the Christian faith… Hence, more than one occurrence is mentioned which it would be difficult to explain by purely natural causes. The limited space at my disposal does not permit of an enumeration of them; but it is enough to state that in the procedure of the venerable Curé d'Ars there is nothing that savours of charlatanism. M. Vianney is another Saint Vincent de Paul, whose charity works wonders… Wherefore, even from a purely material point of view, he is a most valuable man.

In August 1855, the mayor of Ars informed his Curé that he was a Knight of the Imperial Order of the Legion of Honour. Vianney expressed thanks and added: "Since the poor have nothing to gain by it, tell the Emperor, please, that I do not want it." When the decoration arrived, the Curé would not pay the twelve francs postage. The mayor paid it.

Near to the end

Missionary priests were appointed to help with confessions for the nearly 100,000 pilgrims in the Curé's last year. He began to have fainting spells. "My head gets confused." Once he sat down in his housekeeper's kitchen: "Ah! My poor Catherine, I can do no more." On Easter Day, 24th April 1858 he complained that six parishioners had not made their communion. "There are still some sinners in the parish. It is necessary that I should go, so that another may convert them." On 23rd June 1859 he was too weak to carry the monstrance in the Corpus Christi procession. In July he puzzled one penitent by telling her that she would return to Ars in three weeks, and he confided to another that he was dying but she must tell no one, to avoid a fuss.

A record heat wave broiled the land. Moving from the western part of the United States to Europe. Vianney contracted a fever but managed to rise at one o'clock in the morning and walked with his lantern to the church for confessions. The lines stretched as far as he could see and by eleven o'clock he paused for a little wine. He tried to begin the catechism, but there was no voice. As the sacristan helped him back to the presbytery, Mademoiselle d'Ars passed by with her whole family. They knelt and he blessed the lady who had helped him from the day of his arrival with his cart of books. At one o'clock the next morning no lantern appeared. He called to Catherine, "It is my poor end." He allowed himself to be laid on a soft mattress. The youth of the parish stretched wet canvass on the roof of the stifling presbytery. Various officials arrived and baskets of medals were hauled in to be blessed. Priests made their confessions at his bedside and in the stone silent village the only sound was a small bell which rang each time he tried to raise his hand in absolution.

Asking for his soutane, he took out his last thirty-three francs to pay the physician. Then he whispered to his curate Toccanier that there would be enough money within three years for a new church, without a lottery. He made his confession and in the afternoon twenty priests processed with the Blessed Sacrament for his last communion. "How kind the good God is! When we are no longer able to go to him, he himself comes to us." Bishop Chalandon arrived in time to embrace him. On 4th August there was a violent thunderstorm and, as lightning crashed, the priest Monnin recited, "May the holy angels of God come to meet him and conduct him into the holy city Jerusalem." At these words, the Curé d'Ars died, without any movement or expression on his face.

Last farewell

Inside the packed church, hundreds of candles were reflected on the metal heart of the statue of the Immaculate Conception in which was the ribbon with the names of his first parishioners written with his own hand.

At five o'clock in the morning the body was carried downstairs and placed on a board. People began to file past in an uninterrupted stream lasting two days. At noon the body was carried outside to be photographed for the first time. He had not allowed himself to be photographed in life. Once when the sculpter Cabuchet had tried to copy his features in a ball of wax in the back of the church, Vianney chased him out. Now the mayor did the best he could and placed the Legion of Honour on the body of the man who had called himself a poor soldier.

The news spread fast. In nearby Villefranche, an unmoved freethinker said it was a pity that Vianney had disturbed the nineteenth century.

It is often, and wrongly, said that Vianney was the first parish priest to be canonised. There have been others, from Fortunatus, Ostian, Amabilis and Severus in the early centuries and William of Pontoise, Ivo Helory and John Nepomucene in the middle ages, to Adrian Hilvarenbeck, Nicholas Janssen and Peter Fourier in later times, though none was so completely identified with his parish or did so many routine things so well for so long.

The Requiem was on Sunday, with a procession of 300 priests and religious and 6,000 pilgrims. Jean-Marie-Baptiste Vianney had been shepherd of souls in Ars for forty-one years, five months, and twenty days. Walking directly behind the coffin was Antoine Givre who once heard the Curé d'Ars say to him: "You have shown me the road to Ars. I shall show you the road to Heaven."